S0-ACU-603

TIAN DAYTON

Getting in the Christmas Spirit

A GIFT OF INSPIRATION FOR THE HOLIDAYS

Library of Congress Cataloging-in-Publication Data

©2007 Tian Dayton

ISBN # 978-1-4276-2614-1

Sweet Symbols, its logos and marks are trademarks of
Sweet Symbols, Inc. and Innerlook, Inc.

Publisher:
Sweet Symbols, Inc.
A subsidiary of Innerlook, Inc.
262 Central Park West
New York, New York 10024

EVERY TIME WE LOVE, EVERY TIME WE GIVE, IT'S CHRISTMAS.

-DALE EVANS

Getting in the Spirit

The spirit of the holiday season is surrounding me; everywhere I look I see it. It reminds me that this is a time of year to reaffirm life, family and friendship; to create special moments, carved out of ordinary time, that reconnect me with my self and those around me. The rituals that are part of the holiday season move me and remind me of what's really important. They help me to take a closer look, to appreciate the blessings that are always there, but I forget to notice. The holiday wakes up my senses. I see, smell, taste, touch and hear the season. Lights are flickering everywhere, and I am filled to the brim with inviting smells, music, laughter and special foods. This year I will allow myself to enjoy the holiday season in all of its rich variety, knowing that just as it may occasionally try my endurance; it will also nourish my spirit. I will let the rhythm of the season in; I will get in the spirit.

I allow the spirit of the holiday season to be with me

JOY IS NOT IN THINGS; IT IS IN US.

-BENJAMIN FRANKLIN

Having Fun

Today I will have fun. I'll take delight in little things, roll with the holiday energy and let go a little. This is a time of year to step out of my ordinary routines and let something new enter my world. There is music in the streets and a lilt in the atmosphere. There are celebrations, services and parties that are here for me to enjoy. I remember how much I used to love the holidays as a child when everything felt magical and alive and the world transformed before my eyes into a wonderland filled with spicy smells, fudge and Christmas decorations. When I couldn't wait to do the next thing. Today I'll let the child in me play and get exited. When I forget to let go and have fun I lose something very important, when I forget to play, I miss something very necessary to living an enjoyable life. Everybody needs to have light hearted fun, to rekindle and renew their own spirit.

Today I will have a little bit of my own fun.

IF YOU SURRENDER COMPLETELY TO THE MOMENTS AS THEY PASS, YOU LIVE MORE RICHLY THOSE MOMENTS.

-ANNE MORROW LINDBERGH

The Spaces in Between

Some of my happiest holiday moments aren't necessarily the big events or the parties or even the holiday itself. They are the spaces in between. Walking down a decorated street hearing holiday music wafting on the air, a lit outdoor Christmas tree that I didn't expect to see, wrapping presents while listening to Christmas carols or cooking and getting ready to welcome people. The spaces in between. The quiet interludes that aren't loaded up with expectations and holiday pressures. The little moments that breathe holiday spirit into an otherwise ordinary day. I will take an extra minute to enjoy and appreciate those moments this holiday season, knowing that happiness isn't what's in a box, but what's around it.

I am with the holiday spirit in little ways

WE ARE ALWAYS GETTING READY TO LIVE BUT
NEVER LIVING.

-RALPH WALDO EMERSON

Try Something New Each Year

Host a Holiday Get Together

Have a Day of Quiet or Meditation at Home

Try a New Recipe

Buy New Christmas Music

Go to a Different Christmas Event or Service

Send out Christmas Cards or Holiday Greetings

Buy Something Special to wear for the Holidays

Take a Holiday Excursion you wouldn't have taken otherwise

YOU ATTRACT TO YOU THE PREDOMINANT THOUGHTS THAT
YOU ARE HOLDING IN YOUR AWARENESS, WHETHER THOSE
THOUGHTS ARE CONSCIOUS OR UNCONSCIOUS.
THAT'S THE RUB.

-MICHAEL BERNARD BECKWITH

Appreciating What I Have

Today I will appreciate all the gifts that come my way each and every day. I have the gift of life. I have love and friendship. I have the ability to recognize the beauty that surrounds me. I am rich in spirit. I understand that the more I appreciate what I already have, the more what I have can grow. When I focus on what isn't there, that's what I create more of. When I focus on what's there, something mysterious happens. What I love and appreciate expands. Anything alive needs to be cared about and appreciated to thrive whether it's a plant, an animal or a person. The universe is alive too. I will appreciate it so that it can grow in my gaze, expand in my presence.

I see this alive and abundant universe for what it is

On Giving

YOU GIVE BUT LITTLE WHEN YOU GIVE OF YOUR POSSESSIONS.

IT IS WHEN YOU GIVE OF YOURSELF THAT YOU TRULY GIVE.

FOR WHAT ARE YOUR POSSESSIONS
BUT THINGS YOU KEEP AND GUARD FOR FEAR
YOU MAY NEED THEM TOMORROW?

IS NOT DREAD OF THIRST WHEN YOUR WELL IS FULL,
THIRST THAT IS UNQUENCHABLE?

THERE ARE THOSE WHO GIVE LITTLE OF THE MUCH
WHICH THEY HAVE -
AND THEY GIVE IT FOR RECOGNITION AND THEIR
HIDDEN DESIRE MAKES THEIR GIFTS UNWHOLESOME.

AND THERE ARE THOSE WHO HAVE LITTLE AND GIVE IT ALL.

THESE ARE THE BELIEVERS IN LIFE AND THE BOUNTY OF LIFE, AND
THEIR COFFER IS NEVER EMPTY.

THERE ARE THOSE WHO GIVE WITH JOY,
AND THAT JOY IS THEIR REWARD.AND THERE ARE THOSE WHO GIVE WITH PAIN,
AND THAT PAIN IS THEIR BAPTISM.

AND THERE ARE THOSE WHO GIVE AND KNOW NOT PAIN IN GIVING,
NOR DO THEY SEEK JOY, NOR GIVE WITH MINDFULNESS OF VIRTUE;

THEY GIVE AS IN YONDER VALLEY THE MYRTLE BREATHES
ITS FRAGRANCE INTO SPACE.

THROUGH THE HANDS OF SUCH AS THESE GOD SPEAKS, AND FROM
BEHIND THEIR EYES HE SMILES UPON THE EARTH.

IT IS WELL TO GIVE WHEN ASKED, BUT IT IS
BETTER TO GIVE UNASKED, THROUGH UNDERSTANDING........

THEREFORE GIVE NOW, THAT THE SEASON OF GIVING MAY
BE YOURS AND NOT YOUR INHERITORS'.

YOU OFTEN SAY,
"I WOULD GIVE, BUT ONLY TO THE DESERVING."

THE TREES IN YOUR ORCHARD SAY NOT SO,
NOR THE FLOCKS IN YOUR PASTURE.

THEY GIVE THAT THEY MAY LIVE, FOR TO WITHHOLD IS TO PERISH......

-KAHLIL GIBRAN

THE LEAST OF THINGS WITH A MEANING IS WORTH MORE IN
LIFE THAN THE GREATEST OF THINGS WITHOUT IT.

-CARL JUNG

Giving With an Open Hand

Today I will recognize that when I give with one hand and take with the other, I am not in the Christmas spirit. Christmas is about giving with an open heart, giving gifts of the spirit. In my busy life, I can forget how important it is to just take time to be in the moment. I forget that the secret to enjoying life is to appreciate what I have. I will remind myself today that God's presence is right here, right now. God has given me life and created a world full of beauty and abundance in which I am meant to live that life fully. Giving with an open hand is aligning myself with God, with the generosity of spirit.

I give freely

Embrace the spirit of giving

Gifts of the Spirit

1.

Bake or make something for someone

2.

Pay attention to someone who feels forgotten

3.

Give a gift to someone new

4.

Volunteer to help somebody

5.

Take a child on a tour to look at the holiday decorations

6.

Take someone who needs something special, out for a meal

HAPPINESS CANNOT COME FROM WITHOUT. IT
MUST COME FROM WITHIN. IT IS NOT WHAT WE SEE
AND TOUCH OR THAT WHICH OTHERS DO FOR US
WHICH MAKES US HAPPY; IT IS THAT WHICH WE THINK
AND FEEL AND DO, FIRST FOR THE OTHER FELLOW
AND THEN FOR OURSELVES.

-HELEN KELLER

Giving Myself Presents

I will take extra good care of myself today. Only I know what really, really pleases me. I will allow myself those quiet pleasures in my day, knowing that when I nourish and care for myself in all these little ways, it has big reverberations inside of me. My ability to feel enjoyment, relies on the many tiny ways I care for myself. If I skip over these, if I wear myself out unnecessarily, withhold tiny pleasures that would be just as easy to let myself have, I create a backlog of need. Then I want something big to make me feel better. But even when I get it, the pleasure doesn't last. My good feelings about life and this season rest more on a thousand tiny moments that one or two big ones.

Life is in this moment,
the holiday is in this moment.

AT CERTAIN MOMENTS, ALWAYS UNFORSEEN,
I BECOME HAPPY... I LOOK AT THE STRANGERS
NEAR AS IF I HAD KNOWN THEM ALL MY LIFE...
EVERYTHING FILLS ME WITH AFFECTION...
IT MAY BE AN HOUR BEFORE THE MOOD PASSES,
BUT LATELY I SEEM TO UNDERSTAND THAT
I ENTER UPON IT THE MOMENT I CEASE TO HATE.

-WILLIAM BUTLER YEATS

Golden Moments

I have moments during the holidays when life feels heightened. I look around whatever room I'm in and have another kind of a vision of what life is really about. I stop and drop beneath the surface, I see things differently, I experience the deeper meaning of life.

Life is more than it appears to be

People are often unreasonable, illogical, and self-centered;

Forgive them anyway.

If you are kind, people may accuse you of selfish, ulterior motives;

Be kind anyway.

If you are successful you will win some false friends and true enemies;

Succeed anyway.

If you are honest and frank, people may cheat you;
Be honest and frank anyway.

What you spend years building, someone could destroy overnight;
Build anyway.

If you find serenity and happiness, they may be jealous;
Be happy anyway.

The good you do today, people will often forget tomorrow;
Do good anyway.

Give the world the best you have, and it may never be enough;
Give the world the best you've got anyway

You see, in the final analysis, it is between you and God;
It was never between you and them anyway.

THE GREAT BLESSINGS OF MANKIND ARE WITHIN US
AND WITHIN OUR REACH; BUT WE SHUT OUR EYES,
AND, LIKE PEOPLE IN THE DARK, WE FALL UPON
THE VERY THING WE SEARCH FOR,
WITHOUT FINDING IT.

-SENECA

There is Music in the Air

There is music in the air. There is joy in the streets. There is a lilt in people's steps. Even through the exhaustion, the over doing it and the gift giving mania, people are still reaching out to each other in little and big ways. I am reminded this holiday season of the basic goodness of people. I see it in people's eyes. We are all striving to be happy in whatever way we know how. Trying to feel good, to make sense of our lives. To feel like we have a meaningful place in the scheme of things. Today, I will quietly bless others on their journey knowing that every blessing I give, I create first in my own mind and heart. Even the thought of blessing someone spreads a little light in me.

I wish people well

WHEN I STARTED COUNTING MY BLESSINGS,
MY WHOLE LIFE TURNED AROUND.

-WILLIE NELSON

Opening to Receive

Today I open my mind and heart to receive what God is sending me. I will not turn away. I will not ward off my own good because I cannot take it in or out of fear or because it seems too easy. Life is meant to be full. The universe just keeps going. I am the one who sets artificial limits. I understand that receiving is another kind of giving. If I cannot open my heart and take life in, I will never feel full. I will insult the giver by not appreciating what they are trying to give me. It is blessed to give and it is also blessed to receive, sometimes, they are the same open channel.

I can take life In

THE BEST THINGS IN LIFE ARE NEAREST. BREATH IN YOUR
NOSTRILS, LIGHT IN YOUR EYES, FLOWERS AT YOUR FEET,
DUTIES AT YOUR HAND, THE PATH OF RIGHT JUST BEFORE YOU.
THEN DO NOT GRASP AT THE STARS, BUT DO LIFE'S PLAIN,
COMMON WORK AS IT COMES, CERTAIN THAT DAILY DUTIES
AND DAILY BREAD ARE THE SWEETEST THINGS IN LIFE..

-ROBERT LOUIS STEVENSON

It Is What it Is

I have waited for these days with excitement and anticipation. There has been a build up to this season. I will remind myself that this season need not meet any magical expectations in order to be OK. The real miracle has already happened. I am alive and in touch with the living universe that is always surrounding me waiting for me to see it. I understand that I am a child of God and that I have a place in this world. I accept that even death cannot destroy my soul, that some part of me will live forever. This is a moment in the year to reaffirm my commitment to life. Today and every day, I will respect and appreciate the life I've been given.

I accept the holiday I am being given

I HAVE FOUND THAT AMONG ITS OTHER BENEFITS,
GIVING LIBERATES THE SOUL OF THE GIVER.

-MAYA ANGELOU

Thinking of Others

Today I recognize that we are all children of God. In just the same way that I can have a personal relationship all my own with God, so can everyone else. Each of us stands in our own shaft of divine light. The person I may be worrying or even obsessing about has their own Higher Power, and it's not me. Curiously, this awareness allows me to take the behavior of others less personally, to recognize others as separate people. They are probably doing the best that they can just as I am. I stretch my mind into their reality and intuit what might be going on for them. When I really take time to consider the needs, wishes and dreams of others, my understanding grows and so does my compassion. When I allow others to have their own divine guidance, I feel more trusting of the universe and I release both of us from my own overpreoccupation. I can do something *for* another person but I cannot do something *as* them. They have their own will and they have a right to exercise it in ways that feel right to them.

I see past the surfaces

IT IS BETTER TO LIGHT ONE CANDLE THAN CURSE
THE DARKNESS.

- CHRISTOPHER SOCIETY MOTTO,
THE SENTIMENT OF AN OLD CHINESE PROVERB

Lighting One Candle

I will do what I can today. My contribution to society may not earn me a Nobel Prize or fame or wealth, but it is what I have to give. Why should I hold back my contribution because I don't feel it is as worthy or significant as another person's? Though someone else may have seemingly more to give, it is simply what they have to offer. Let them give it and let me contribute in my own way. Every sensitive generous act is worthy.

Sometimes the sweetest gifts are smiling at someone who feels forgotten or listening to a person who is in pain. These are gifts of the spirit, of the self, and they are significant. When I give of myself, I give something everlasting-something that can be carried in the heart and spirit of another person, something that cannot be destroyed by the elements. I give a piece of eternity.

I will light one candle

A tourist visiting Italy came upon the construction site of a huge church.

'What are you doing?'
he asked three stonemasons who were working at their trade.

'I'm cutting stone,'
answered the first tersely.

'I'm cutting stone for twenty lire a day,'
the second responded.

'I'm helping build a great cathedral,'
the third stonemason announced."

-**FROM AND I QUOTE**

WE DO NOT RECEIVE WISDOM,
WE MUST DISCOVER IT FOR OURSELVES, AFTER A
JOURNEY THROUGH THE WILDERNESS WHICH NO ONE ELSE
CAN MAKE FOR US, WHICH NO ONE CAN SPARE US, FOR OUR
WISDOM IS THE POINT OF VIEW FROM WHICH WE COME
AT LAST TO REGARD THE WORLD..

-MARCEL PROUST

Recovering the Spirit
that's Already Within Me

Today I recover the spirit that has always been there, vibrating just beneath the surface of my being. I am whole and in tact. I call to that part of me that has been waiting patiently for me to come to my senses and claim it. That part of me that is eternal, that never dies. Spirit has been with me even in my darkest hours. I turn and look, I quiet my mind and see, I rest in awareness and experience. Spirit has never been far, but I have been asleep. Today I wake up to spirit.

I will learn to see what is already there

On Forgiveness

A MIDDLE-AGED MAN CAME TO PLACE HIS CHILD IN ONE OF MY CLASS-
ES, BUT I REALIZED I HAD NO ROOM AT ALL. I LOOKED AT THIS MAN AND
IMMEDIATELY KNEW. THIS WAS THE GUARD WHO HAD BEATEN ME NINE
YEARS BEFORE.

A SPIRIT CAUGHT ME. I UNDERSTOOD THAT I HAD TO FIND SPACE FOR HIS
BOY. I COULD NOT REPEAT THE HARM THAT HAD BEEN DONE TO ME. I ASKED
HIM, "DO YOU KNOW ME?" HE SAID, "NO." I ASKED HIM IF HE REMEMBERED
A NIGHT IN JULY OF 1956. JUST THEN, THE MAN LOOKED AT MY FACE AND
STARTED CRYING. HE BEGAN TO WALK AWAY, BUT I STOPPED HIM, SAYING,
"WAIT, I'LL TAKE THE CHILD. I HAVE CARRIED SCARS FOR YEARS, BUT I HAVE
FORGIVEN YOU ALL THOSE THINGS." THAT MAN MIGHT HAVE LEFT ME PER-
MANENTLY DISABLED, BUT IN ALLOWING ME TO HELP HIS BOY, HE MADE ME
FEEL FULFILLED IN WHAT I WANTED TO DO FOR YOUNG PEOPLE.

-RECOUNTED BY JOEL KINAGWI, FROM THE MEANING OF LIFE

THERE'S NOTHING SADDER IN THIS WORLD
THAN TO AWAKE CHRISTMAS MORNING AND NOT BE A CHILD.

- ERMA BOMBECK

Receiving Through a Child's Heart

I open to receive the wonderment of the holiday season. I will look through the eyes of the child in me at the beauty of the season. Lights flicker, people sing and gather and give each other gifts. I will accept this decorated world as a personal present, created just for me to enjoy. I will be uncomplicated, open, ready to laugh and take pleasure in whatever seems pleasurable. Just because I am an adult doesn't mean I cannot allow the child within me to experience the excitement of the holiday season as it weaves its magic around me.

I will look through the eyes of the child within me.

LOVE IS NOT AUTOMATIC. IT TAKES CONSCIOUS PRACTICE
AND AWARENESS, JUST LIKE PLAYING THE PIANO OR GOLF.
HOWEVER, YOU HAVE AMPLE OPPORTUNITIES TO PRACTICE.
EVERYONE YOU MEET CAN BE YOUR PRACTICE SESSION..

- DOC CHILDRE AND SARA PADDISON

The Spirit of Giving

I will love others today before I wait for others to love me. I will give generously of my warmth and good opinion. Rather than make others prove themselves worthy of my affection, I will recognize that the simple act of caring about people, warms my own heart.

An open heart is an opened heart

On Caring For Others

I BELIEVE THAT THE VERY PURPOSE OF LIFE IS TO BE HAPPY. FROM THE VERY CORE OF OUR BEING, WE DESIRE CONTENTMENT. IN MY OWN LIMITED EXPERIENCE I HAVE FOUND THAT THE MORE WE CARE FOR THE HAPPINESS OF OTHERS, THE GREATER IS OUR OWN SENSE OF WELL-BEING. CULTIVATING A CLOSE, WARMHEARTED FEELING FOR OTHERS AUTOMATICALLY PUTS THE MIND AT EASE. IT HELPS REMOVE WHATEVER FEARS OR INSECURITIES WE MAY HAVE AND GIVES US THE STRENGTH TO COPE WITH ANY OBSTACLES WE ENCOUNTER. IT IS THE PRINCIPAL SOURCE OF SUCCESS IN LIFE. SINCE WE ARE NOT SOLELY MATERIAL CREATURES, IT IS A MISTAKE TO PLACE ALL OUR HOPES FOR HAPPINESS ON EXTERNAL DEVELOPMENT ALONE. THE KEY IS TO DEVELOP INNER PEACE

-THE DALAI LAMA

THERE IS NO REALITY EXCEPT THE ONE CONTAINED WITHIN US. THIS IS WHY SO MANY PEOPLE LEAD SUCH AN UNREAL LIFE. THEY TAKE THE IMAGES OUTSIDE THEM FOR REALITY AND NEVER ALLOW THE REALITY WITHIN THEM TO ASSERT ITSELF.

- HERMANN HESSE

My Personal Holiday

I will enjoy my holiday close in this year. Enjoy doing the simple things that give me pleasure whether that is decorating a tree and enjoying it throughout the season, cooking little holiday goodies and sharing them with friends or listening to my favorite Holiday music. I will make my home feel warm and welcoming. And then I will let it welcome me, each day throughout the season. My home is my haven. A place where I can be relaxed and free. Where I can create whatever environment suits me best. Where I can curl up and feel quiet pleasure. Much of my enjoyment of the holiday is simply letting in the holiday atmosphere I create as I wander around my own little world.

I enter the spirit of Christmas

ISN'T IT FUNNY THAT AT CHRISTMAS SOMETHING
IN YOU GETS SO LONELY FOR -
I DON'T KNOW WHAT EXACTLY,
BUT IT'S SOMETHING THAT YOU DON'T
MIND SO MUCH NOT HAVING AT OTHER TIMES.

- KATE L. BOSHER

Holiday Melancholy

Today I feel melancholy for Christmases past. I have images of warm get togethers, people floating through my mind, holidays that have happened but have changed over the years. I find myself longing for things gone by. I suppose that is a natural part of the holidays, too. To romanticize the past. Memory is a funny thing, it creates all these warm pictures and leaves out the frayed edges. But today, I want to wind the clock back even if only in memory. I will remind myself that everything gone by is still a part of me, still mine, in a way. I will recollect it with gratitude for having had it rather than regret that it is no longer with me.

I remember with a tinge of bittersweet longing

The
23rd
Psalm

The Lord is my shepherd; I shall not want.

He maketh me to lie down in green pastures:
He leadeth me beside the still waters.

He restoreth my soul:
He leadeth me in the paths of righteousness for
His name's sake.

Yea, though I walk through the valley of the shadow of
death, I will fear no evil: for thou art with me; thy rod and
thy staff they comfort me.

Thou preparest a table before me in the presence of
mine enemies: thou anointest my head with oil;
my cup runneth over.

Surely goodness and mercy shall follow me all the days
of my life: and I will dwell in the house of the Lord
for ever.

STRESS IS THE BODY AND MIND'S RESPONSE TO ANY
STRESSFUL PRESSURE THAT DISRUPTS THE BALANCE IN THE
MIND OR BODY. IT OCCURS WHEN OUR PERCEPTIONS
OF EVENTS DON'T MEET OUR EXPECTATIONS AND WE DON'T
MANAGE OUR REACTION TO THE DISAPPOINTMENT. AS A
RESPONSE, STRESS EXPRESSES ITSELF AS RESISTANCE,
TENSION, STRAIN OR FRUSTRATION, THAT THROWS OFF OUR
PHYSIOLOGICAL AND PSYCHOLOGICAL EQUILIBRIUM,
KEEPING US OUT-OF-SYNC AND STRESSED-OUT.

- DOC CHILDRE AND HOWARD MARTIN

Holiday Intensity

The holidays bring all sorts of feelings for me. They heighten everything. Everything gets a bit more intense. Holidays make expectations run so high, everything is supposed to be cheerful all the time. Sometimes in the holiday intensity I get ahead of myself. I over do it. I forget that this is a time for extra self awareness and care not less. I get scared of my own intensity, I over react to myself, I feel like a bouncing ball with no center. Today, I will consciously find my center when I lose it.

I take actions to reduce my stress

WORRY GIVES A SMALL THING A BIG SHADOW.

-SWEDISH PROVERB

Prioritizing

I'm going to make certain that I get the down time I need this season. Holidays are exhausting no matter how you cut it, so this season I'm going to do only what's necessary. I'll put off till the New Year whatever is postponable and relax and enjoy the merriment and celebration. I'll plan ahead with present buying and wrapping so I don't get myself into a last minute bind where I have to grab anything I see and stay up late wrapping. I know that when I feel relaxed I enjoy seeing people more. When I'm rested the extra holiday activities go more smoothly. If I get enough rest and down time, I'll be less edgy and when the little things go wrong that inevitably go wrong over the holidays, I'll have an easier time letting them roll off my back.

Prioritizing around the holidays is critical to my enjoyment of them

REMEMBER THAT YOUR THOUGHTS ARE THE PRIMARY CAUSE OF EVERYTHING. SO WHEN YOU THINK A SUSTAINED THOUGHT IT IS IMMEDIATELY SENT OUT INTO THE UNIVERSE. THAT THOUGHT MAGNETICALLY ATTACHES ITSELF TO THE LIKE FREQUENCY, AND THEN WITHIN SECONDS SENDS THE READING OF THAT FREQUENCY BACK TO YOU THROUGH YOUR FEELINGS. PUT ANOTHER WAY, YOUR FEELINGS ARE COMMUNICATION BACK TO YOU FROM THE UNIVERSE, TELLING YOU WHAT FREQUENCY YOU ARE CURRENTLY ON. YOUR FEELINGS ARE YOUR FREQUENCY FEEDBACK MECHANISM.

-JACK CANFIELD

My Thoughts Have Power

I will be aware of what I think this season. The thoughts that go through my mind have a creative power. They affect me, they affect others and they affect my life. My mind is like a laboratory in which I experiment with life scenarios. I try things out in my imagination, then I put them into action. I can create a positive environment within my mind to live in, that will affect my world.

I will think carefully and thoughtfully today

THE HEROINE'S [AND HERO'S] JOURNEY IS AN INDIVIDUAL QUEST. TRAVELING THIS PATH, THE HEROINE MAY FIND, LOSE AND REDISCOVER WHAT HAS MEANING TO HER, UNTIL SHE HOLDS ONTO THESE VALUES IN ALL KINDS OF CIRCUMSTANCES THAT TEST HER. SHE MAY REPEATEDLY ENCOUNTER WHATEVER THREATENS TO OVERCOME HER, UNTIL FINALLY THE DANGER OF LOSING HER SELFHOOD IS OVER.

-JEAN SHINODA BOLEN

Embracing the Void

There is emptiness as well as fullness to the holiday season. Today I will embrace them both. I will see the emptiness as a spiritual void that is actually full in a completely different sort of way. A God shaped hole. When I allow myself to embrace my own inner emptiness rather than run from it, a paradox happens. What was unknown becomes known, what was frightening becomes tolerable and what was empty becomes full. The void I feel inside of me is really a spiritual wilderness. When I enter it barren trees flower and bear fruit. It is alive and vibrating. It sooths and sustains me and I feel tingly inside.

There is a world within me waiting to awaken

SAYING THANK YOU IS MORE THAN GOOD MANNERS.
IT IS GOOD SPIRITUALITY.

-ALFRED PAINTER

I Thank You God

I will say 'thank you God' today each time something happens that feels nice. If I enjoy my cup of tea in the morning, I will say 'thank you God." If I see a quarter on the sidewalk I will pick it up and thank God. If someone smiles at me in a way that feels good, if the sun feels warm on my back, if my car starts, my dinner is there or someone in my life is with me for another day, I will say "thank you", recognizing that these are all blessings. By the end of the day, I will have thanked God for a lot of things. I will have remembered what makes my life worth living. I will have increased my conscious contact with the source of all good.

I recognize the small daily blessings of life

EVERYBODY TODAY SEEMS TO BE IN SUCH A TERRIBLE RUSH;
ANXIOUS FOR GREATER DEVELOPMENTS AND GREATER
WISHES AND SO ON; SO THAT CHILDREN HAVE VERY
LITTLE TIME FOR THEIR PARENTS; PARENTS HAVE VERY LITTLE
TIME FOR EACH OTHER; AND THE HOME BEGINS THE
DISRUPTION OF THE PEACE OF THE WORLD.

-MOTHER TERESA

Home for the Holidays

I will value my home today. I will take time for those I love. I know that my time is the most valuable thing I have to give. Our world runs at a fast pace, we are all on a track to get somewhere but, at the end of the day, where are we all going in such a rush? What am I looking for so hard in the future that makes it worth running right by my present?

I slow down so I can see and value what surrounds me

THEN, WITHOUT REALIZING IT, YOU TRY TO IMPROVE
YOURSELF AT THE START OF EACH NEW DAY; OF COURSE,
YOU ACHIEVE QUITE A LOT IN THE COURSE OF TIME.
ANYONE CAN DO THIS, IT COSTS NOTHING AND IS
CERTAINLY VERY HELPFUL. WHOEVER DOESN'T KNOW IT
MUST LEARN AND FIND BY EXPERIENCE THAT A QUIET
CONSCIENCE MAKES ONE STRONG.......... HOW WONDERFUL
IT IS THAT NOBODY NEED WAIT A SINGLE MOMENT
BEFORE STARTING TO IMPROVE THE WORLD

-ANNE FRANK

Remembering to Take Care of Myself

Today is a day to be reborn into the life I already have. To see and value it differently. To cherish it knowing that it is mine only for a while. I am God's gift to me. God has lovingly placed my life into my own hands to care for. God means for me to cherish and care for my own life in each and every way. I am responsible for what I do with me and what I do with my life. In caring for me, I am loving God's world. I am showing love and respect for what God has put into my hands until I rest once again in God's arms for all of eternity.

I value the gift of my own life

OUR DEEPEST FEAR IS NOT THAT WE ARE INADEQUATE. OUR DEEPEST FEAR IS THAT WE ARE POWERFUL BEYOND MEASURE. IT IS OUR LIGHT, NOT OUR DARKNESS, THAT MOST FRIGHTENS US. WE ASK OURSELVES, WHO AM I TO BE BRILLIANT, GORGEOUS, TALENTED, FABULOUS? ACTUALLY, WHO ARE YOU NOT TO BE? YOU ARE A CHILD OF GOD. YOUR PLAYING SMALL DOES NOT SERVE THE WORLD. THERE IS NOTHING ENLIGHTENING ABOUT SHRINKING SO THAT OTHER PEOPLE WON'T FEEL UNSURE AROUND YOU. WE WERE BORN TO MAKE MANIFEST THE GLORY OF GOD THAT IS WITHIN US. IT IS NOT JUST IN SOME OF US; IT IS IN EVERYONE. AS WE LET OUR OWN LIGHT SHINE, WE CONSCIOUSLY GIVE OTHER PEOPLE PERMISSION TO DO THE SAME. AS WE ARE LIBERATED FROM OUR OWN FEAR, OUR PRESENCE AUTOMATICALLY LIBERATES OTHERS

-MARIANNE WILLIAMSON

READ BY NELSON MANDELA IN HIS 1994 INAUGURAL ADDRESS

BLESSED IS THE SEASON WHICH ENGAGES THE WHOLE
WORLD IN A CONSPIRACY OF LOVE.

-HAMILTON WRIGHT MABIE

To Every Season, There is a Reason

Life is about learning to let go and the older I get the more I have to let go of, because so many experiences are behind me. But letting go doesn't mean that they never happened. Nor does it mean they are no longer mine. I am a tapestry of all that has happened for me over the years. A living history of my own life. Today I will take time to consciously remember and honor all that has gone by. I give thanks for all my life and I respect myself for having come this far. I send a message of love and forgiveness, I say a silent prayer for all those who have joined me on this journey, for all those I have walked with over both the rough and the smooth terrain of my life. You are all a part of me, you live in my heart, you give me a feeling of fullness in my life.

I love the life I have been given

Pueblo
Blessing

HOLD ON TO WHAT IS GOOD
EVEN IF IT IS A HANDFUL OF EARTH.

HOLD ON TO WHAT YOU BELIEVE
EVEN IF IT IS A TREE WHICH STANDS BY ITSELF.

HOLD ON TO WHAT YOU MUST DO
EVEN IF IT IS A LONG WAY FROM HERE.

HOLD ON TO LIFE
EVEN WHEN IT IS EASIER LETTING GO.

HOLD ON TO MY HAND
EVEN WHEN I HAVE GONE AWAY FROM YOU.

WHEN WE THINK OF LOSS, WE THINK OF THE LOSS,
THROUGH DEATH, OF PEOPLE WE LOVE. BUT LOSS IS A FAR
MORE ENCOMPASSING THEME IN OUR LIFE. FOR WE LOSE
NOT ONLY THROUGH DEATH, BUT ALSO BY LEAVING AND
BEING LEFT, BY CHANGING AND LETTING GO AND MOVING
ON. AND OUR LOSSES INCLUDE NOT ONLY OUR SEPARATIONS
AND DEPARTURES FROM THOSE WE LOVE, BUT OUR
CONSCIOUS AND UNCONSCIOUS LOSSES THROUGH ROMANTIC
DREAMS, IMPOSSIBLE EXPECTATIONS, ILLUSIONS OF FREEDOM
AND POWER, ILLUSIONS OF SAFETY-AND THE LOSS OF OUR
OWN, YOUNGER SELF. THE SELF THAT THOUGHT IT WOULD
ALWAYS BE UNWRINKLED AND INVULNERABLE
AND IMMORTAL.

-JUDITH VIORST

Necessary Losses

Over the holidays I sometimes feel melancholy for people who are no longer around. Life is full of gains and losses, they are inevitable but I feel their loss more keenly during these days when family and friends gather. I recall what the holidays felt like when they were here. I will say a quiet prayer of appreciation for all that they have been to me and I will ask for the strength to go on without them in my daily life. And I will recognize that remembering them is honoring their spirit and what they meant to me. No one is ever really lost if I hold them in my heart. When I hold them with love, I feel full rather than empty. I feel blessed by their presence in my heart rather than punished by their absence. Or maybe a little of both, but holding them with appreciation lets the memory of them feel alive and nourishing.

I remember those I've loved with love

On Giving

Henry Wadsworth Longfellow was filled with sorrow at the tragic death of his wife in a fire in 1861. The Civil War broke out the same year, and it seemed this was an additional punishment. Two years later, Longfellow was again saddened to learn that his own son had been seriously wounded in the Army of the Potomac. Sitting down to his desk, one Christmas Day, he heard the church bells ringing.
It was in this setting that Longfellow wrote these lines:

I heard the bells on Christmas Day
Their old familiar carols play,
And wild and sweet
The words repeat
Of peace on earth, good will to men!

And thought how, as the day had come
The belfries of all Christendom
Had rolled along
The unbroken song
Of peace on earth, good will to men!

Till, ringing, singing on its way,
The world revolved from night to day,
A voice, a chime,
A chant sublime
Of peace on earth, good will to men!

Then from each black, accursed mouth
The cannon thundered in the South,
And with the sound
The carols drowned
Of peace on earth, good will to men!

It was as if an earthquake rent
The hearth-stones of a continent,
And made forlorn
The households born
Of peace on earth, good will to men!

And in despair I bowed my head;
"There is no peace on earth," I said;
"For hate is strong
And mocks the song
Of peace on earth, good will to men."

Then pealed the bells more loud and deep.
"God is not dead, nor doth he sleep!
The wrong shall fail,
The right prevail,
With peace on earth, good will to men!"

-PULPIT HELPS, 12-92

A MAN WHO BECOMES CONSCIOUS OF THE RESPONSIBILITY HE BEARS TOWARD A HUMAN BEING WHO AFFECTIONATELY WAITS FOR HIM, OR TO AN UNFINISHED WORK, WILL NEVER BE ABLE TO THROW AWAY HIS LIFE. HE KNOWS THE "WHY" FOR HIS EXISTENCE, AND WILL BE ABLE TO BEAR ALMOST ANY "HOW"... IT DID NOT REALLY MATTER WHAT WE EXPECTED FROM LIFE, BUT RATHER WHAT LIFE EXPECTED FROM US. WE NEEDED TO STOP ASKING ABOUT THE MEANING OF LIFE, AND INSTEAD TO THINK OF OURSELVES AS THOSE WHO WERE BEING QUESTIONED BY LIFE- DAILY AND HOURLY. OUR ANSWER MUST CONSIST, NOT IN TALK AND MEDITATION, BUT IN RIGHT ACTION AND IN RIGHT CONDUCT. LIFE ULTIMATELY MEANS TAKING THE RESPONSIBILITY TO FIND THE RIGHT ANSWER TO ITS PROBLEMS AND TO FULFILL THE TASKS WHICH IT CONSTANTLY SETS FOR EACH INDIVIDUAL

-VICTOR FRANKEL TALKS ABOUT HOW HE SURVIVED LIFE IN THE CONCENTRATION CAMPS OF WORLD WAR II

Healing at the Holidays

The holidays can be a time for healing if I want to look at them that way. The seasons and its rituals bring up feelings in me. Some of the feelings are tainted with melancholy but they are none the less healing to feel. If I experienced pain and loss, hiding it won't help anything. I will trust God and myself to give me the strength to just let my feeling happen, knowing that it is in feeling them that I can heal them, that I can elevate them to a conscious level where I can reflect on them and draw meaning from them. I can learn the lessons they are meant to teach me. Then I will free up emotional space to let the sense of connection and the affirmation of caring seep into my pores and fill me with those soothing emotions.

The holidays are healing

THE TRUTH IS THAT OUR FINEST MOMENTS ARE MOST LIKELY
TO OCCUR WHEN WE ARE FEELING DEEPLY
UNCOMFORTABLE, UNHAPPY, OR UNFULFILLED. FOR
IT IS ONLY IN SUCH MOMENTS, PROPELLED BY OUR
DISCOMFORT, THAT WE ARE LIKELY TO STEP OUT OF OUR RUTS
AND START SEARCHING FOR DIFFERENT WAYS OR TRUER
ANSWERS.

-M. SCOTT PECK

Bah Humbug

What do I do with my negative feelings around the holidays? They seem so out of place. I feel like I'm not supposed to have them. But they are their any way, tugging at the corners of my mind or casting a gray pall over the activities of my day. I want to get rid of them but there they are. Today I will try something different. I will just let them be, I will stop fighting them. I will just feel them through. Feelings have a life cycle of their own, just like a flower. They have a seed, they grow, they flower and become full and then they slowly dissipate and whither away. Whether they are positive or negative feelings they have this cycle. Because feelings are just feelings, they come and go. They aren't permanent or even lasting. They only gain power when I fight them. When I accept them and let them be, they are just like the flower, they bud, flower fully and then the petals fall.

I let my feelings run their course

ONE'S REAL LIFE IS SO OFTEN THE LIFE THAT
ONE DOES NOT LIVE.

-OSCAR WILDE

Decorating My Own Life

    I will create a welcoming holiday atmosphere in my own home. The holidays are a great excuse to put a little extra fun and energy into creating beauty, wonder and pleasure right where I live. I will remember how magical it felt as a child to see a decorated Christmas tree, or flickering candles and lights. How warm and welcoming the smells from baking and cooking all the traditional holiday foods felt to me. Today, I will create that for myself and those I love. The holidays are right at my fingertips, waiting for me to touch them, to bring them to life. I will show my family that it's worth creating a beautiful home just for them and the family and friends we share.

I can create holiday warmth and good will
...right where I live

Simple
Gifts

'Tis the gift to be simple,
'Tis the gift to be free,
'Tis the gift to come down where you ought to be,
And when we find ourselves in the place just right,
It will be in the valley of love and delight.

When true simplicity is gained,
To bow and to bend we shan't be ashamed.
To turn, turn will be our delight,
'Til by turning, turning we come round right

'Tis the gift to be loved and that love to return,
'Tis the gift to be taught and a richer gift to learn,
And when we expect of others what we try to live each day,
Then we'll all live together and we'll all learn to say,

'Tis the gift to have friends and a true friend to be,
'Tis the gift to think of others not to only think of "me",
And when we hear what others really think and really feel,
Then we'll all live together with a love that is real.

-SHAKER ELDER JOSEPH BRACKETT, JR.

FORGIVE ALL WHO HAVE OFFENDED YOU,
NOT FOR THEM, BUT FOR YOURSELF.

-HARRIET U. NELSON

Forgiveness

Today I recognize forgiveness as the quickest road to freedom and serenity. When I forgive my past, I release myself from the grip that it has on my present. I no longer carry that heavy baggage around with me. It is difficult to live in peace today if I am psychically engaged in yesterday's battles. But I cannot forgive and release what I do not first feel and come to terms with. The type of forgiveness that bypasses this stage only pays lip service to letting go. I will do what I need to do today to process fully the issues in my life that remain unresolved so that I can let them go.

I meet my inner world honestly and with integrity.

WE DON'T SEE THINGS AS THEY ARE, WE SEE THEM AS WE ARE

-ANAÏS NIN

It's Just a Season

This year, the holidays don't have to look a certain way in order to be acceptable to me. I will let them unfold. I'll look at them as a time to get together with friends and family but I won't build them up so much in my mind that they overwhelm me. This year I will recognize that holidays are just days. I don't need to load them up with expectations that make them feel burdensome. I can just let them be whatever they are. When I insist that the holidays go a certain way, I set myself up for disappointment. I lose my spontaneity and start to dread things rather than look forward to them. There is so much going on every where I turn that I might as well just enjoy the ride. This year the holidays can just be a season. And this year, I can just roll along with them and be part of whatever comes along with no particular need for things to be any certain way.

I will allow the holiday season to move along easily

Prayer

MAY TODAY THERE BE PEACE WITHIN. MAY YOU TRUST GOD THAT YOU ARE EXACTLY WHERE YOU ARE MEANT TO BE. MAY YOU NOT FORGET THE INFINITE POSSIBILITIES THAT ARE BORN OF FAITH. MAY YOU USE THOSE GIFTS THAT YOU HAVE RECEIVED, AND PASS ON THE LOVE THAT HAS BEEN GIVEN TO YOU. MAY YOU BE CONTENT KNOWING YOU ARE A CHILD OF GOD. LET THIS PRESENCE SETTLE INTO YOUR BONES, AND ALLOW YOUR SOUL THE FREEDOM TO SING, DANCE, PRAISE AND LOVE. IT IS THERE FOR EACH AND EVERY ONE OF US.

-SAINT THERESA'S PRAYER

Little Gifts
to Give
Myself

Breathe Deeply

Place your hand where you can feel the gentle rise and fall of your belly as you breathe. Breathe in slowly. Pause for a count of three. Breathe out. Pause for a count of three. Continue to breathe deeply for one minute, pausing for a count of three after each inhalation and exhalation. This brings the nervous system back into balance.

Take a Rest

Researcher Thomas Wehr at the National Institute of Mental Health conducted studies during which he had people lie down in a quiet, darkened room for fourteen hours each night, conditions similar to those under which we evolved during the millions of years before the discovery of artificial light. Under these conditions, the subjects reported a state of pleasant relaxation coupled with a crystal clear consciousness. Also, while they were in these states of relaxation and clarity, their pituitary glands were releasing prolactin, a mood soother, into their blood streams.

Take a Bubble Bath

A warm bath is a quick way to get a shot of prolactin. Research shows that heat causes prolactin to be released into the bloodstream. Prolactin is that natural soothing body chemical that we often associate with nursing mothers. It causes us to feel calm, soothed and serene.

Take a Walk or Exercise

Exercise releases serotonin into the blood stream. This is a natural mood elevator as well as a mood regulator. Find a form of exercise that you find enjoyable and relaxing.

SOON SILENCE WILL HAVE PASSED INTO LEGEND.
MAN HAS TURNED HIS BACK ON SILENCE. DAY AFTER
DAY HE INVENTS MACHINES AND DEVICES THAT
INCREASE NOISE AND DISTRACT HUMANITY FROM THE
ESSENCE OF LIFE, CONTEMPLATION, MEDITATION...
TOOTING, HOWLING, SCREECHING, BOOMING, CRASHING,
WHISTLING, GRINDING, AND TRILLING BOLSTER HIS EGO.
HIS ANXIETY SUBSIDES. HIS INHUMAN VOID SPREADS
MONSTROUSLY LIKE A GRAY VEGETATION.

-JEAN ARP

Meditation

Today I draw strength and nourishment from within. I will meditate. There is a medicine chest inside of me if I tap into it. I have body chemicals that are meant to smooth me out, to nourish me and let me feel good inside. I can get those going through quiet and meditation. I can feel them coursing through my system, elevating my mood. In my own inner quiet, I will look for nothing. I will simply be. I will bear witness to the inner workings of my mind but I will not tell my mind to do or be anything. I will just let it flow and float in and out of consciousness. I will just be

I breathe in and I breathe out

SUCCESS IS NOT ABOUT GETTING IT DONE. IT IS ABOUT
STILL DREAMING AND FEELING POSITIVE IN THE UNFOLDING.
THE STANDARD OF SUCCESS IN LIFE IS NOT THE MONEY OR
THE STUFF-THE STANDARD OF SUCCESS IS ABSOLUTELY
THE AMOUNT OF JOY YOU FEEL.

-ESTHER AND JERRY HICKS

Success

This season I am filled with feelings of treasuring life for no good reason other than that I am aware that it's a gift. When I can appreciate the gift of life, of the holiday season, it automatically deepens my experience of it. Suddenly the moment goes from hum drum to having a quiet sort of grace. I am willing to be truly successful today to feel joy in my own unfolding. To take pleasure and look forward to the activities of my day. This is how I measure success. Not by how much surrounds me but by how much capacity I have to enjoy what's around me. I am not here forever. Why should I wish away the circumstances of my life? Today, I will measure my success as a person by how much I am able to love the grace that is all around me.

I experience joy

THE HOLIEST OF HOLIDAYS ARE THOSE
KEPT BY OURSELVES IN SILENCE AND APART;
THE SECRET ANNIVERSARIES OF THE HEART.

-HENRY WADSWORTH LONGFELLOW

Creating My Own Rituals

Rituals ground me in my own day. My morning tea, my walk through the park, dinner with my family. These are the daily rituals that give my life a sense of continuity and solidity. They hold me, they bond me with those I love. The Holidays are full of rituals. Yearly rituals that deepen my sense of life and remind me of what's really important. Just experiencing another holiday season, decorating another tree, having holiday meals with family and friends is part of what gives meaning to my year. Part of what gives my life its symmetry. I need these rituals to help me remember what to value. They connect me with myself, my memories, my family and friends. And they join me with life, with the feeling of what we're all really made of under the skin. Rituals speak in their own voice and today, I am listening.

I respect the importance of rituals in my life

RESPONSIBILITY DOES NOT ONLY LIE WITH THE LEADERS
OF OUR COUNTRIES OR WITH THOSE WHO HAVE BEEN
APPOINTED OR ELECTED TO DO A PARTICULAR JOB.
IT LIES WITH EACH OF US INDIVIDUALLY. PEACE, FOR
EXAMPLE, STARTS WITHIN EACH ONE OF US. WHEN WE
HAVE INNER PEACE, WE CAN BE AT PEACE WITH
THOSE AROUND US

-HH THE DALAI LAMA

Staying Calm

Peace begins with me. I need to remember that emotions run high during the holidays. My joys are higher and my longings are stronger. The world is more intense than it usually is. When I forget this, I start to feel out of step if I'm not cheerful and happy all the time. I want to push away my inner world and I get a little afraid of what I'm experiencing if it doesn't fit my image what I'm supposed to be feeling given the merriment of the season. Then I engage in a cover up, but the only person I am covering up is me. When I do that, I am only half there. Today I will let myself have my full range of feelings around the holiday, knowing that they may, at times, be a bit of a roller coaster, but knowing also, that I will land comfortably at the end of the ride.

I accept the emotional intensity of the holiday season

WE MUST NOT, IN TRYING TO THINK ABOUT HOW WE CAN
MAKE A BIG DIFFERENCE, IGNORE THE SMALL DAILY
DIFFERENCES WE CAN MAKE WHICH, OVER TIME, ADD UP TO
BIG DIFFERENCES THAT WE OFTEN CANNOT FORESEE.

-MARIAN WRIGHT EDELMAN

Taking a Quiet Moment

I am full today. I feel the warmth of the holidays surrounding me. I am blessed to be alive and I am full of that holiday good feeling. Warm, relaxed. Things are finally happening, the anticipation is over and I can relax and enjoy it. Whatever didn't happen yet, I can let go of. I will pick it up next year God willing. But for this moment, it is enough. I feel that sense of renewing bonds with friends and family. That affirmation of mutual caring and affection. That sense of meaning something special to people and people feeling special to me. I breathe in this lovely feeling of connection and goodness in life. This is what the holidays are for, a chance to pause and count my blessings. A chance to feel a quiet sense of gratitude for another year of living. It's good to be alive.

I breathe in the spirit of the holidays

PEOPLE USUALLY CONSIDER WALKING ON WATER OR
IN THIN AIR A MIRACLE. BUT I THINK THE REAL MIR-
ACLE IS NOT TO WALK EITHER ON WATER OR IN THIN
AIR, BUT TO WALK ON EARTH. EVERY DAY WE ARE
ENGAGED IN A MIRACLE WHICH WE DON'T EVEN REC-
OGNIZE: A BLUE SKY, WHITE CLOUDS, GREEN LEAVES,
THE BLACK, CURIOUS EYES OF A CHILD -- OUR OWN
TWO EYES. ALL IS A MIRACLE.

-THICH NHAT HANH

Joy

Today I will embrace the experience of joy. The real purpose of life isn't to grab and get, to preen and try to out do the next guy. The real purpose of life is to deepen my ability to experience joy. Joy is the gift. Joy is the accomplishment. Joy is what fills me up. When I am able to feel joy, I don't need to chase around trying to get the world to admire and envy me on the outside because I feel empty on the inside. When I feel joy, I am happy in my own life because I understand that it is the only one that is actually mine to live, the only one through which I can connect with spirit.

Joy is its own reward

THANKS TO MY MOTHER, NOT A SINGLE CARDBOARD BOX HAS FOUND ITS WAY BACK INTO SOCIETY. WE RECEIVE GIFTS IN BOXES FROM STORES THAT WENT OUT OF BUSINESS TWENTY YEARS AGO.

-ERMA BOMBECK

Holiday Memories

    I will wrap myself in holiday memories today. I will recall that wonderful feeling of excitement I had as a child, the sense of wonder at watching the world transform into something rare and magical. I will remember the way it felt to go to relative's and friend's houses for festive times together. I'll picture people in warm and contented holiday moods. Everyone has some special holiday moments to recall. I have them too, tucked safe in my heart just where they belong. Today I will take one out, hold it, look at it and let it warm my heart.

I remember what makes me glow inside

Dad lost his job at the gypsum mine after getting into an argument with the foremen and when Christmas came that year we had no money at all. On Christmas Eve, Dad took each one of us out into the desert night one by one...."Pick out your favorite star," Dad said that night. He told me I could have it for keeps. It was my Christmas present. "I want that one," I said.

Dad grinned, "That's Venus," he said. Venus was only a planet he went on, and pretty dinky compared to the real stars. She looked bigger and brighter because she was much closer than the stars. Poor old Venus didn't even make her own light, Dad said. She shown only from reflected light. He explained to me that planets glowed because reflected light was constant, and stars twinkled because their light pulsed.

"I like it anyway," I said. I had admired Venus even before that Christmas. You could see it in the early evening, glowing on the western horizon, and if you got up early, you could see it in the morning, after all the stars had disappeared.

"What the hell," Dad said. "It's Christmas. You can have a planet if you want."

And he gave me Venus.

"Years from now, when all the junk is broken and long forgotten," Dad said, "you'll still have your stars."

From The Glass Castle by Jeanette Walls

WHOSOEVER WISHES TO KNOW ABOUT THE
WORLD MUST LEARN ABOUT IT IN ITS PARTICULAR DETAILS.
KNOWLEDGE IS NOT INTELLIGENCE.
IN SEARCHING FOR THE TRUTH BE READY
FOR THE UNEXPECTED.
CHANGE ALONE IS UNCHANGING.
THE SAME ROAD GOES BOTH UP AND DOWN.
THE BEGINNING OF A CIRCLE IS ALSO ITS END.
NOT I, BUT THE WORLD SAYS IT: ALL IS ONE.
AND YET EVERYTHING COMES IN SEASON.

-HERAKLIETOS OF EPHESOS

One with Spirit

Today I let go and align my will with the Spirit that surrounds me constantly. When I willfully try to push my life in place or make myself feel and be some idea of what is right, I tie Spirit's hands. And I am limited in my vision. Today I invite Spirit to involve itself intimately in all the petty arrangements of my life. I am one with Spirit and so nothing is too small for Spirit to be a part of. There is no separateness. Separateness in only an illusion. The very second I invite Spirit to be with me, Spirit is there.

I let go and let God

BOTH ABUNDANCE AND LACK EXIST SIMULTANEOUSLY IN OUR LIVES, AS PARALLEL REALITIES. IT IS ALWAYS OUR CONSCIOUS CHOICE WHICH SECRET GARDEN WE WILL TEND... WHEN WE CHOOSE NOT TO FOCUS ON WHAT IS MISSING FROM OUR LIVES BUT ARE GRATEFUL FOR THE ABUNDANCE THAT'S PRESENT- LOVE, HEALTH, FAMILY, FRIENDS, WORK, THE JOYS OF NATURE AND PERSONAL PURSUITS THAT BRING US PLEA-SURE- THE WASTELAND OF ILLUSION FALLS AWAY AND WE EXPERIENCE HEAVEN ON EARTH.

-SARAH BAN BREATHNACH

Love What You Have

Today I will love what I have rather than always wanting something to be different before I allow myself to be happy. There is so much in my life right now. When I sit still and allow the life I already have to surround me, there is a feeling of fullness that begins to expand inside of me. When I spend all my time chasing what I think I need in order to be happy, I am never still enough to actually experience this feeling of contentment. Contentment is available to me all the time if I am willing to slow down and allow it to come into me. My happiness has more to do with loving what I already have than regretting or chasing after what I don't have.

Today I will love the life I already have

Let us not keep Christmas

Let me not wrap, stack, box, bag, tie, tag, bundle, seal,
keep Christmas. Christmas kept is liable to mold.
Let me give Christmas away, unwrapped, by exuberant
armfuls. Let me share, dance, live Christmas
unpretentiously, merrily, responsibly with overflowing
hands, tireless steps and sparkling eyes.

Christmas given away will stay fresh—
even until it comes again

-LINDA FELVER

GOD DOES NOT DIE ON THE DAY WHEN WE CEASE TO BELIEVE
IN A PERSONAL DEITY, BUT WE DIE ON THE DAY WHEN OUR
LIVES CEASE TO BE ILLUMINED BY THE STEADY RADIANCE,
RENEWED DAILY, OF A WONDER, THE SOURCE OF WHICH IS
BEYOND ALL REASON

-DAG HAMMARSKJOLD

Standing in Awe

I will stand in awe today. I will let the mystery of life move and inspire me. I will fill my soul. When I can open myself and just be with the peace that passes all understanding I am uniting myself with the power of the now. I am tuning in to the creative mind that breathes life into each and every aspect of our universe. Today I will not back up from the intensity of life. I will let the energy of the universe live inside of me. I will be in the moment.

I see the beauty that is mine

IN EVERYONE'S LIFE, AT SOME TIME, OUR INNER FIRE GOES
OUT. IT IS THEN BURST INTO FLAME BY AN ENCOUNTER WITH
ANOTHER HUMAN BEING. WE SHOULD ALL BE THANKFUL FOR
THOSE PEOPLE WHO REKINDLE THE INNER SPIRIT.

-ALBERT SCHWEITZER

A Christmas Affirmation

Life is a gift. Everywhere we look, we see evidence of God's creative power. In this season I will remember where I truly come from. I will remember that my place is to stand in awe of the divine mystery, to recognize, celebrate and praise all the beauty that surrounds me constantly, waiting for me to notice it. Today we open our hearts to receive the blessing of God's love, here on earth. As I open my heart to divine love and guidance I become purposeful, my life becomes meaningful and my world feels safe and warm. I respect and appreciate the life that I have been given and place my heart and day into the loving hands of my Higher Power

I appreciate the mystery of the season

LAY NOT UP FOR YOURSELVES TREASURES UPON EARTH,
WHERE MOTH AND RUST DOTH CORRUPT, AND WHERE
THIEVES BREAK THROUGH AND STEAL: BUT LAY UP FOR YOUR-
SELVES TREASURES IN HEAVEN, WHERE NEITHER MOTH NOR
RUST DOTH CORRUPT, AND WHERE THIEVES DO NOT BREAK
THROUGH NOR STEAL: FOR WHERE YOUR TREASURE IS, THERE
WILL YOUR HEART BE ALSO

-MATTHEW 6:19-21

Think on These Things

ABOUT THE AUTHOR

Dr. Tian Dayton is a psychologist and writer. She is the author of more than fifteen self books and a well known national speaker. One of the hallmarks of her extensive writings has been its emphasis on personal growth, spiritual inspiration and motivation. These gift books represent the fulfillment of a project dear to the author's heart. They integrate both Tian's best-selling affirmations with the wise voices of all those who have inspired her through the years. The author has been blessed with her husband Brandt of more than three decades and their two adult children Marina and Alex. She hopes that you enjoy reading these books as much as she has enjoyed writing them.

Other Sweet Symbols Gift Books

On Your
Special Day

A beautifully written and designed little book filled with nourishing and motivating "messages to the self" for a very special day. *A Birthday Celebration* is rich with affirmations, quotes and readings that touch the heart and ignite the spirit. The perfect way to tell someone you care; to say "Happy Birthday" from the heart.

Sharing the
Journey of a Lifetime

On mothering provides support, guidance and information in order to to help mothers do their very important and demanding job. Deeply inspiring readings and expert advice make the perfect gift for Mother's Day, a baby shower or just to appreciate a Mom you know. A book any mother would cherish.

Being Together
Day by Day

An elegant collection of affirmations, readings and quotes to inspire tenderness and affection in those who read it. This gift book affirms and celebrates the power and presence of love. *On Loving Someone* motivates us to believe in caring and connection, and to recognize the importance of love in our daily lives.

To Order:

More of Dr. Dayton's line of inspirational
gift books from Sweet Symbols:

LOG ONTO:

Amazon.com
Barnes and Nobel.com
Sweet Symbols.com

For bulk, party or corporate orders
please email info@sweetsymbols.com

Also visit sweetsymbols.com for beautiful,
downloadable cards and gift tags for all occasions
with inspirational messages

Sweet Symbols the Gift of Inspitation